When You're Deep in a Thing

Also by Anthony Cappo:

My Bedside Radio

When You're Deep in a Thing

Anthony Cappo

Four Way Books
Tribeca

For my mother, Helen Cappo, with love and gratitude

Library of Congress Cataloging-in-Publication Data

Names: Cappo, Anthony, author.
Title: When you're deep in a thing / Anthony Cappo.
Description: New York : Four Way Books, [2022]
Identifiers: LCCN 2022003860 | ISBN 9781954245273 (trade paperback) | ISBN
9781954245334 (epub)
Subjects: LCGFT: Poetry.
Classification: LCC PS3603.A6675 W48 2022 | DDC 811/.6--dc23/eng/20220201
LC record available at https://lccn.loc.gov/2022003860

This book is manufactured in the United States of America and printed on
acid-free paper.

Four Way Books is a not-for-profit literary press. We are grateful for the assistance
we receive from individual donors, public arts agencies, and private foundations
including the NEA, NEA Cares, Literary Arts Emergency Fund, and the
New York State Council on the Arts, a state agency.

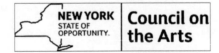

[clmp]

We are a proud member of the Community of Literary Magazines and Presses.

Contents

iv.

v.

vi.

Notes

KINDLING

after Stanley Kunitz

My mother never forgave my father for
leaving. But that's an old story.

Let's talk about wind ghosting
through the basement, rains

buckling its floor. On the porch,
swarms of pests. Her left optic nerve

severed, her light halved.
All apertures shrinking, she withdrew—

a cherry macerating
in its own tears, pieces shedding

at alarming speed. The house,
in sympathy, cast off its beams.

When the last slat thudded,
we gathered what was left

and torched it.

Saturday Night Fever

My mother couldn't afford to buy me a leather jacket,
but my sister's cop boyfriend gave me a John Travolta
haircut. His training: *When someone does something
to this body, I pay attention.* He took me hunting—

shooting at deer illegally from a moving car. I cried
when they broke up. He taught me how to drink,
how to slam the door when you walk in a room
to show you're badass.

I was a strobe—my dad gone—pulsing
in the dark. Teachers said I'd changed. It's easy
to be cruel with a tough guy haircut
and gold rope chain. My sister's disco

throbbing on the lunchroom jukebox,
I'd sit with the greasers, but minutes would pass
in silence. Slinked away or just waited for the bell.
I always thought it was about the music but

it wasn't.

PURGATION

After confession, I felt light as a cherub.
My body skipping, burden of sin
expelled from my soul so blackened

but now clear again—
like a long-time smoker's lung
suddenly pink

at the wave of a doctor's hand.
So if hit by a car, or kidnapped
and killed by one of the bad men

lurking about, I could float in heaven
with the popes and my grandparents.
But I backslid—fought with my sister,

talked back to my mom,
cursed, trouble at school. God
watching always.

AUBADE

Slack as dumbwaiters, we wake,
whispering in slanted light.

Jaws droop like lanyards strung
from our faces. Too soon this ice bucket

gut punch, this wretched call to work.
I slide my hand up and down your back—

desire sluicing through. Your head on my pillow
thawing decades of fierce-clung ice.

And the fear? Right—my glue-and-chewing-gum self
spalling on the floor. Another crumble,

another's wind-swept force. But we're coupled
and I'm intact—bulwark against a marauding world.

Our morning idyll broken, we dress
and brave the day. These moments receding

with each shirt pulled over our heads. We freeze
the pixels dissolving in our minds.

Roll them around as comfort and fuel
for the next time—our bodies once more

twined together.

Thank you to whomever

planted the pink tulips
in the flower beds
under the just-blooming
trees on Gansevoort Street.
Bright, fulsome, swaying
in the breeze—petals the size
of my palm. Three beds in a row,
framed by metal edging with spikes
like helmets of World War I German soldiers.
Taller flowers peek above the rest
like baby chicks popping out
of their shells. Some with petals missing,
exposing the yellow pistil, stamen,
ovaries. Showing procreation can thrive
even in the midst of pandemic.
But even in this brilliance, this magic, I still hear
the ambulances cranking up their sirens—
soundtrack of the streets of late.
On sidewalks, no faces, only eyes
bordered by masks. Reminder
that even in a world with beauty
not everything is going to be alright.
Grateful even more for this pastel shock,
so unexpected, that shook me out of my head,
made me gasp a deep breath.

Sitting in a Beach Café in Tulum in the Last Hours of the Obama Administration

Look homeward, but a thorn's
       in my eye. The braying

in the capitol a foghorn
       shouting down all

that's decent and kind. Old wine
       in old thin skin.

And here in Mexico, single again,
       stitching pieces of my life—

fissured, worn, resist being put back
       together. A child's ragdoll

thrown out a window. Strung
       from the rafters like a quisling king

after liberation. And in Washington
       gilded pageantry, staggering lies.

My Facebook feed reads
       like an online guestbook

for a dear departed. Our parting president
        says we will survive this,

but I shiver. Dread leaching through
        like toxic sludge. The hole

in my life matching the one
        in our state. We will resist,

but things can unravel
        like a cheap red tie. We try,

but the brown-boot creature
        in the rearview can overtake.

All we have is a patched-up Ford
        and a pedal. We floor it, hoping

for enough juice to outrun
        its storming pursuit.

GATE C31

Sitting in seat 16B, belt too tight, overhead light on,
thinking about loss. About my friend Jen, and how
we traveled for work together for years—Seattle,
Asheville, Boise, Missoula. So many times
whooshing through airports—check-ins, bag weighs,
pat-downs. Battled ice storms, turbulence, delays—
killing time in out-of-the-way places. Haven't traveled
together in years, but still think of her every time I fly.
I'll text her—*no traffic, easy security, bag only 34 pounds!*

And I think of my dad—sick, declining, surely in his final
years, months, weeks. Wonder if there's anything I still want
to say or ask. I've said so much. The divorce, absence, lack
of support. Sad furrow running through my childhood.
Ground tilled so thoroughly, it seems nothing more
could grow. (And yet, sometimes, my anger.)
I wonder what was going on. All those nights out
even when still with my mother. Were there flings,
one-night stands, relationships? Did he almost leave
years before he did?

And I think about a whole world of loss, so foreign to me
even in my fifties. I'm lucky—both parents alive.
(Our *hardy peasant stock*, my friend would say.)

A couple of acquaintances gone, but
it's strange. So much pain, so little
mortal loss.

I know it's coming. Dark freight train devouring
fuel, pistons whirring, picking up steam.
I'm not remotely ready. Soft body not even near
the tracks, but it will find me. When it does
I'll flatten like a cartoon under a paving machine.
All I can do is lay me down and take the blow.

They say grief comes in waves, and if so,
a tsunami's approaching my skiff. I'm an open vessel—
grief, loss, have at me. I'll recover, but sadder,
wiser—maybe. Try to make sense. And where
to put all this love?

Walter S.

Deposition, September 8, 2015, Olympia, Washington

I used to like to work in the garden.
That was one of my main deals, is working
in the garden, and I can't do that anymore.
Anyway, shoot. I don't know what to tell you.
I had a lot of things we did together
that we can't do now. It's different.
Life is different when you're dying.

I know I'm funny, but I'm not trying to be.
And I love everybody around me,
but I can't do a thing
about coming back. I've got to go
and I know it.

My wife does everything for me. She's
unbelievable. Unless I have her,
then I've got to call in hospice,
and I don't want to do that unless
I absolutely have to, because
they keep shoving pain pills down me,
and I don't necessarily want to feel better,
I just want to be loved. That's all.

Pillbug

On my knees, I roust weeds
  from their dug-in
nests. Roots screech
  reluctant goodbyes,
and carry a tiny armadillo creature
  yanked from earth's
core. Slumber interrupted,
  he wipes his eyes, scrambles
to the surface. Crawls on my hand,
  threatens a jag
up my arm. But really just scared.
  World upended, so much done,
undone. So many steps
  to retrace. Collapses
his body in a clenched-shut case
  like any pillbug—
or person—would do.

Window Seat

I wish I had GPS or something
to tell me what city is the cluster
of lights on this side of Lake Michigan.

What road is that glowworm highway
slinking beside the curling river?
To connect what I see to some song,

some story, a news piece I've read.
Then blazes of light would mean more
than just Wendy's and big-box districts

down here. CVS, Rite Aid, Walgreens—
the whole pharmacopoeia of strip mall
sprawl America. An arrow in the right direction,

our dots revealed on the graph. The where
to the impossible why.
The earth's a whirling pincushion.

Electric gashes scar the ground,
drilling rigs bore through strata,
pumpjacks suck out what's left.

We walk bereft, bracing our insides
together. Crave firm beneath feet,
dirt girding toes, a watcher

above us watching. Not just
frost on our windows, sound
of jet engines screaming.

When you're deep in a thing

and that thing has an anvil
that sinks in your chest and

squeezes your thoughts
down trap door corridors

when a walk in the street
is a gauntlet of faces

the only song
a suite of dirges

you visit the Falls
and think not

of their beauty
but their promise

to sweep you away
lean over a railing

at the Niagara River
and imagine joining

its rush as it tumbles
toward the edge or

back in the city

drive over a bridge

see a pedestrian
walkway and wonder

if there's a ledge
below to stop

a leap and you hope
(for future reference)

there isn't
when you're deep

in a thing it's good
to have people

who love you
faces in your heart

you wouldn't want to see
shattered

Come Blow Your Horn

This pretty girl Roberta Love—no lie—
I'd go to her house hang out some
she had a boyfriend but

seemed interested
we were 15 or 16   I was
reading this book

about Frank Sinatra   my dad
had split for his love pad
and me all puffed up

with Frank's exploits
if you want to score—roar!
not going to be weak or beg

in front of any girl
or boy and now a *take it or leave it bitch*
kind of guy   I played it

real hard   she dropped me
real easily and soon
her boyfriend looking for me

and I'm shaking
it's amazing
how far you can get

from yourself

SUGGESTIBLE

And—*hush-hush*—you'll say something
that'll take decades to uncoil. *Take this worm
and eat it.* Some idea that nestles deeper
than I know, dark sticky mist on all it touches.
A story to turn me out of orbit.
Some ought, some should, some wrong
to make good. A rule about boys
and girls. Mere raise of eyebrow
or voice. The ocean gets rolled
by the tides, sundew seduces the fly.

I NEVER FEEL SO SEXLESS

as at my mother's house—
Thanksgiving, Christmas,

my four sisters circling, dad
miles away again. Memories

of hangdog childhood seep in
like methane. Duck-and-cover

years screen on reels
of nitrate film.

I take a shower—hot water
enveloping—think about my ex,

her incendiary hair, and feel a swell.
I look down and am startled

at this thing growing
between my legs—this interloper,

patched-on appendage God forgot
to erase. Somewhere outside

a whole me walks about.
But here ghosts whisper, frames

fade to shame.

FUNERAL

In St. Magdalene's, light shines through
the blue stained-glass, through sweet
incense the priest swings over the casket
and the holy water he sprinkles in final blessing.
Behind him scenes from the saint's life—
washing Jesus's feet while the jealous disciples
glare, greeting the risen Messiah on the road,
wound bursting red from his side. At the altar,
Jesus slouches wooden on the cross,
gazing at the words written over the doors:
Nor Do I Condemn You—Go and Sin No More.

As the priest says Jesus walks with the deceased, I see
a candle in the nave quiver. It calms, but I'm transfixed,
staring for signs this movement was coincidence.
And now I lean on his words, thinking
maybe this is my call, my time to be felled
by the gospel's fire. Seven demons leap
in my throat.

In high school at Stacy Berman's, all sex
and nerves, I swear I saw Jesus's face
reflected in a window across the street.

She wasn't a believer, but was kind
and didn't deny my vision.

The priest assures the mourners that in God's house
there are many dwelling places,
and the deceased is surely in one.

Lord, I am not worthy to receive you
but only say the word and I shall be healed.

The service continues and the candle wavers again.
And again—random, swept by currents. No sign
of the long finger of the Lord; no onramp to the road
to Damascus. I exhale and return to my secular distress.

Soon I'll be at the cemetery hearing last words,
holding a baby rose to lay over the coffin,
soft thorns sharp enough to jab but not enough
to prick. But for now I'm in the procession,
orange flag stuck to the top of my rental car, running
every stop sign, every red light.

Not Fade Away

Hi, honey. I know you're pissed
I call you that—we're over and all—
but sometimes I can't resist. I read

that psych wards ban aspartame
cause it aggravates anxiety,
so maybe you should look into that,

just saying? But sweetness, you were always
so xenial with me, which is a million dollar
way of saying hospitable, welcoming,

receiving. And no, that is not a reference to sex.
Mostly. But truth, I think about sex with you
all the time. Remember, baby—our bodies

flesh-fired rockets! My thew has undergone
a blue freeze since I left you. How stupid of me.
Maybe we could work on a thaw? I'm sure

I'm not helping my cause, but darling,
how I'd love to hear the bell and ta-da!
you're at my door. I'm a mess

but there must be something
you miss?

Tiny Life

Message me
if

you have a big
life

her profile
says

Well that's great
but I'm tired

of trying to live
a big life

I want a tiny life
a quiet

wake up and walk
in the park

life not clenching
my teeth

in the dark
life

some peace not
self-

flagellation a
connection

with someone
would be nice

life

INDEPENDENCE DAY

Descartes thought the pineal gland the principal seat
of the soul, and, if true, Joe's soul exploded
when the third bullet hit its mark. Was Victor suffering

from dementia, some buildup of brain sand
when he fired the shots?
No. Victor did not have dementia or any other brain funk.

He was drunk, true, an old punk in full-on
mess mode. He ached for Anna, who was through
with him. *A violent fuck of a man*, she said.

He toddled into the theater, Glock held high,
and demanded three things: a gold watch, canary, and a plane
to Cuba. Waving his gun, he said, *Express train*

to the coroner, right here. Vic shot up the screen
while reciting his screed against modernity. Joe flashed back
to childhood memories of Chief Jay Strongbow

applying his sleeper hold and lunged in Vic's way.
Without delay, Vic fired and Joe joined the legions
of dead 21st-century heroes. They named the theater

after him, the mayor declared a day in his honor,
and his wife got a framed proclamation.
They all talked about what a beautiful soul Joe had.

Identity Theft

The TV ad promises
they'll notify me immediately
as soon as they detect a threat

to my identity. A great relief
because I'm concerned lately—
feel it elongate, detach,

an amoeba splitting
during mitosis. But those fears
are all yesterday. They'll text,

send an electric buzz
through my system the minute
I start to fissure. Then,

like seeing horses sprint
to high ground before
a tsunami, I'll be warned

and can fuse myself together.

REED LAKE

They say the beaver is huge but I haven't seen him.
All week I've crossed Canyon Bridge, scanning
the water, but no sign. Only ducks and crows,
whose grating caws, so close, unnerve me.

At night the bridge lights up, rows of blue orbs
that would soothe if they didn't seem to point
to some surreal, unsettling place. But walking the lake
at day is different. The cawing on the bridge

that sends me scurrying sounds natural
in the teeming green—like pterodactyl cries
rising over a prehistoric swamp. The *shirl*
of the streams calm. Thimbleberries

line the path. On a log, two turtles
sun themselves, looking like shiny black turrets.
Maybe the beaver is afraid of the turtles—
their barrels full of lead. Or maybe he appears

only to the lucky, or those who believe
in him. I want to believe in everything,
anything. Streams of stigmata.
Healing hand of the Lord thwacking me

in the face. To be fastened, connected.
I want to see the beaver

and feel blessed.

SUNSET, ESZTERGOM, 1916
after a photograph by André Kertész

Come with me and I will show you
fissures of men. Truck-sized holes
wishing only to be filled. Beyond
the sunset, a scattering of chimney
smoke. Our boat a scythe
approaching the heart of the river.
The waters lapping the banks whisper
muted revelations. We float
to our appointed course, the sun
a sinking host. We look east
to Mecca, Jerusalem, wherever.

ELIZABETH AND I AT SUNSET

after a photograph by André Kertész

Yes, we will huddle as the mottled sky
falls. As factories sink into the river,
as another winter jabs stiff fingers
into the land. Your head on my shoulder,
our bodies a seamless *No*
against approaching dark. Cold wind
breaches our coats. Our blood
rushes to meet it.

EMPIRE STATE BUILDING, NEW YORK, 1967

after a photograph by André Kertész

Empire down, reflected in sidewalk
puddle. Fallen spire's tip sticks
the pavement like a syringe.
Debris on the ground circles
like biplanes. Tenements,
barred windows obscure
the base. Blackout, Son of Sam
still to come. Studio 54.
I Wanna Be Sedated.

Dancer, Paris, 1926
after a photograph by André Kertész

My father's mother was a flapper,
crashing Philly speakeasies
with her sisters. Makeup, mirrors,
low-cut dresses—the wild side
of the family. My mom's side
stiffer stuff—pious, unsmiling,
fingering rosaries at daily mass.
Carrying around their stern
Sicilian village like a cross. Out
of this piebald mix—me. Spinning
that way, then this. The Bend,
the Twist.

Rainy Day, Tokyo, 1968

after a photograph by André Kertész

Walk between the lines. Follow
a sign and be ghostherded
with a will all your own. Hoist
your umbrella like a shield.
It will protect you from everything
but the streams shooting out
of your own body.

Rainy Day, Paris, 1928

after a photograph by André Kertész

Après le déluge, moi. After
the waters have cleared
the cobbled streets,
sidewalks emptied
into drains. After streetlights
have resumed their stately watch,
I'll remain the same
background figure, head down,
dodging pavement cracks. Rain
drowning the whites of my eyes.

New York, 1972, Twin Towers
after a photograph by André Kertész

Rooster vane, church cross, Twin Towers—
lined up in the rain. Cock crows
the other way while cross
tries to pry the buildings apart.
Space between them like glue
binding two beams. What has been joined
let no man put asunder.

On the Duna, Haraszti, Hungary, 1920

after a photograph by André Kertész

My ragged boatman, an obolus
for your troubles. You steer us steady
from billowy vistas to terminal gate—
a straight journey to our straitened
circumstance. Town mute, trees indifferent—
we have leapt their element. Pulsing sky
has places to go. Darker things
we soon will know.

MELANCHOLIC TULIP, NEW YORK, 1939

after a photograph by André Kertész

How much sustenance

do we need? What

keeps us upright,

heads above

the glass? What

keeps us from drowning

or being scythed by the sea?

Our bodies take arms

against us. We are lead,

we are flower. We

shade from light

into dark. Head first

from a great height,

we hit the ground.

CHEZ MONDRIAN, PARIS, 1926

after a photograph by André Kertész

Apple-shaped vase of flowers, white
table. Straw hat, great coat
hang on thick wooden knobs.
Knotted floor leads
to the stairway bending up
and down. Shadowed
archway just beyond,
just around.

The Great Outdoors

The first time I thought of shooting a man,
I was hunting with my sister's boyfriend, Brian.
A long day—we'd started when it was
dark. By 6 a.m., beer in hand, we were off.
I was 14. Driving an empty highway,
Brian leaned out the window with his shotgun
looking for early-feeding deer, but didn't
see any. We got to the woods
and began walking. He gave me a starter rifle—
one of his old guns, slung across my chest.
Brian meant well—impress my sister,
yes, but took an interest in me.
My dad had just left, my life a weathervane
spinning directionless.

But the forest seemed emptied. Maybe
we were loud, beginner's bad luck.
No deer, no other animals. Disappointed,
I saw some birds in a tree. Didn't come all this way not
to shoot anything, so I aimed and fired
into the branches. The birds flapped away.
My first shot, not even close. Brian laughed—
you'll never get an easier target than that.

The hunt became an hours-long slog.
Dispirited, lagging behind, my weariness
brought myself back to me. I wasn't
the hardened hunter this gun promised.
I wanted to be warm at home with my mom.
Soft, crumbling at first sign of trouble.
Striding far ahead, Brian had discovered
the real me. I could feel it in his smirk.

I wanted to off this tormentor, this dark mirror.
Send him gurgling, staggering. Fill him
with a thousand holes, like Bruce Nauman's
fishes.

But I didn't. Kept walking, head down, a rabbit
without spring. I thought I'd find a new me—granite,
alabaster, steel. But just the usual. No alchemy,
no magic, no hero's journey through dark wood.
We made it back to the car
and drove home. Through the windshield,
the setting sun shone on me
like a spotlight.

All Will Be Revealed

My sister's friend Mark worked at his family's chicken
slaughterhouse in South Philly. He was tall and wore
a cocked newsboy cap like DeNiro

in Godfather II. Lights out, he'd tell ghost stories.
Whisper and float his hands over the candle,
my ten-year-old eyes bulging out of their sockets.

High school graduation my sister threw herself
a party—Mark and other friends came but left early.
She got depressed and drunk on Boone's Farm.

I tried to comfort her—she still had me, I said.
I wasn't what she wanted, but she took me
up on it—kissed my lips, touched

my hips. Only a second, but it sent a shiver
I'd never felt and when I kissed Sue Bell, seventh grade,
she touched me the same way and then I knew.

Larva Migrans

In Morro de São Paolo, they play beach
        volleyball without using
their hands, and an old Portuguese fort
        sits at the tip where
glowing butterflies flit
        over green iguanas,
and hibiscus and angel's trumpet
        fill the most hardened nose.
Glistening waters meet crystal beaches,
        but the sand harbors
a hookworm that burrows under
        feet. And I got one,
and could trace its migration,
        sense it when it moved.
But it never made a path
        to my heart or ate away
at the bedrock that blocks it.
        And I went to a doctor
who gave me a pill to kill it,
        and I swear I felt it
when it died.

Post-Parting

It's still morning
and I've texted three exes,
resurrected my dating profile,
and gathered all my energy
to even think about
leaving my apartment.

I make it to the park to read, to think,
but people near me just blather
on their phones. I want to scream
like Bacon's popes. Babel of voices, none
speaking to me.

I thought I was over this *Solitary Man* shit, but
Here I go again on my own.

A bulldog rests on the thighs
of its owner—owner and girlfriend
in matching Middlebury sweatshirts.
I'd like to find them cute but
all I feel is annoyed. Is it their college spirit,
glowy togetherness? Whatever.
Strangers come up to them and pet

the dog. It's the dog's third
birthday. Happy Birthday, Bulldog.

Hey Bulldog!
Some kind of happiness
is measured out in currency
I don't possess.

I walk down Hudson Street,
couples smiling
having brunch
en plein air
all dewy blah blah.
I know the look, I've had it.
But now it's as ancient
as an AM radio song
I heard on the bus
in grade school.

I keep myself busy—farmer's market,
hardware store, pharmacy.
Back to my place with my bags,
my foraging.

Tail down, I settle in, unpack
my stuff. Wind blows through the open window.
Chill settles everywhere, like a resort town
in autumn. Stores, restaurants close.
Lake gets colder, sprouts icy fingers.

Deep in its frozen dark, I've welcomed
the stillness, respite from
an other's force.
But the lake doesn't get that cold anymore
and neither do I.

I'll shiver, tempt myself
with a weighted descent.
But this time I won't sink. This time
I will not freeze.

Handheld

Deliver us from
isolation. Bring us

pulse reaching
to meet us.

We wait to be
soothed, for news

from the place
where somebody

loves us all.

My Wedding Day

for Sophia Starmack

I couldn't find a mate so I got down on one knee for my Suffering. My bride rode in on a ragged horse, her slackjaw cousins sagging the reins. Her dress weathered, stitched in onyx and pomegranate seeds. My sullen queen of spades. The hall glowed in low candlelight, the priest whispered some words, and it was done. They tried to lift my bride to dance, but the burden too heavy. The band played dirges and Nick Drake. Did we dance the Hokey Pokey? Yes, we did—the Alley Cat and other line dances. My mom clapped with joy; the bride grimaced. And now she's the first breath I feel every morning—entwined arms reminder of our bond. We sway together under the darkest of branches, the murkiest of waters. And when the clocks' rattling chimes demand we kiss, we do.

Paradise

Back when winter was winter, I'd run
home from school warm March days
to see if the bulbs my mother planted
had peeked through the hard-packed dirt

to proclaim we survived another bleakness.
Balm on the way—I couldn't wait to tell her
because it would soften her tense face. She loved
her garden, kneeling like she was pleading

with St. Peter, plucking out weeds, pillbugs,
and other threats to paradise. And I'd like to live
in paradise where everything's peaceful.
No nervous breakdowns hiding behind

couches. No ache from dad absence.
But heaven was eons away. I was just a boy,
weary of this world already, but had to endure
like an Arctic explorer, freeze pelting my face.

A Son Imagines

When the alarm explodes, he wakes and it's still her
draped over him. He braces his body, gropes

for the bathroom. Their kids swarm, scramble
for school. Eggs, grapefruit, a last swig of coffee, and he's gone.

Driving clients all day from office to ranchers to split-
levels. Back to the house for dinner, then out

for the night. Bars, dancers, one-night stands,
the hands that keep him whole. What does he dream

through his smoke rings? What thoughts swirl
through his Scotch and vermouth? Cradling

the whole shaky edifice in his arms. Does he feel
his one life bleeding out his pores? Does he go howling

through the desert, begging for one great passion
to lift him out of the ashes

he's created?

CANTALOUPE (LONG SHADOW OF ABUSE)

I cut a cantaloupe in two. The bottom
of one half so mushy, most of it rotted.
So, like a surgeon, I took my knife,
held the fruit over the trash and cut out
the soft parts, leaving only a thin strip
of orange flesh. Instead of spooning
it out, I leaned over the sink and bit
into it like it was an ear
of corn. Cradling it in my hands, I ate it
with such enthusiasm—juice
dripping down my lips—
that I started moaning and licked
the rind. Smiled sadly
at all the times obsessing over
my sexuality.

Clouds

Looking out my window seat, I see clouds
surveil the Arizona desert, cast Rorschach
shadows on washed-out mounds below.
Gaseous drones roaming at will—track
every lizard and rattler's movement.
Hovering eyes to spy threats to the peace.
Your papers, please.

                        But at first
their blue-black shadows seemed scattered
lake oases breaking the land's monotony.
Pools of hope dotting the desert, stocked
with rainbow trout, perfect for a cool dip
or jet ski.
                But eventually real lakes crawl
across my window—in jagged shapes—
and I know we're not over the desert anymore.
And again clouds are clouds, not benign,
not malignant, no greater significance.

I exit the plane and descend
into the thousand-eyed sunset.

Bodies

That we exist in bodies is ridiculous.
Not the bodies themselves—lattice, torque,
lace—but how soft they are. How everything
can go in a second. Ambulation leads to
ambulance, vehicles to ventilator, hard candy
to coffin. Rocked back with shock, laid up for a week
or eight. The cosmic vacuum is always on and looking
for more specks to lift into oblivion. When my sister
was born everyone said, *Watch out*
for the soft spot on her head. Even then I thought
that was crazy—why would a baby
come so jelled, so open? Everything about her
made me anxious. Every cry, bump, fall
was going to be the end. Fresh torrent of tears—
family shred at the seams.
And now my own body not the given
it once seemed. New medications, dehydration—
routine middle of the night pee now fraught.
Once a body's set in motion downwards, there's no telling
where gravity will deposit it. Gashes, stitches,
displacements. If you're lucky.

And what's the deep meaning of body
fragility? Transience of all things? Supremacy

of soul? Need for pleasure to counter pain?
I'm not wise enough to say.
But when my lover rubs my feet and relief
immediate; when she caresses my back and gives
an unexpected kiss; when we're entwined
and our bodies seamless—all sublime. And far
from ridiculous. This dissociative orphan—
my body—now portal to, yes, pleasure, but also
presence. Safe to exit the head, open senses.
Maybe this is a poem about love, not the body.
But how to separate? A body can glide the path
to love, and love can tether a body to the world.
And now, though my wish is to bound out of bed at night,
I don't. I do what the doctor says—sit at the edge
a couple seconds, stand up but don't walk
right away. Get my bearings. Hold on to things.

Fruit of the Vine

My grandfather sold fruits and vegetables
out of a hearse. It was the Depression,
he got a good deal—lots of cargo room.

Drove that carriage down the street,
stopped at a corner to hawk his wares.
Watermelon on his shoulder, boxes

of the reddest Jersey tomatoes,
blueberries from Vineland, oranges
from Florida. Hustled to keep

the dark shroud from descending
on his family. Produce placed carefully
in the hold, trunk open, curtains

drawn back to reveal the goods.

Work

The backhoe's incisors rip through concrete,
earth, and pieces of old piping. With steely
precision, the operator palms the joysticks.
Smashes old chunks of metal, lifts them

with his digging bucket. All clear, a crew
in fluorescent green vests and hardhats
converge like ground troops
after an aerial bombing. Descend into the hole

with picks, shovels and jackhammers
to finish the mission: dislodge the old piping
they've come to replace. Tape measures flash,
faint smell of something burning. Disturbing

what's settled, settling what's disturbed.
All day like this, and at 4:00 they pack their gear
into the truck. Blue sparks from welding rods
as they seal steel plates over the site.

In the morning—sleep-eyed, coffee cups
steaming—they'll pry them open again.

Dissociation Blues

When I was a kid I could jump my skin
as easily as a ghost skips over a pond. Leap
my mind into some other's eyes and voila!
the world through them. Give the slip
to the pale cadaver tied to my wrist—
heavy guy for a boy to be dragging around.
Another's head's a safe place
to see the world but can't stay.
Back to mine, where it was me,
then not me, then whoever else cared
to sidle in.

I Was the Bully

Tiny punk-ass SOB, hard-edged,
with big friends to back me up. Once
bullied, but now brandishing my own terror—
at awkwards, the unsure, vulnerable.

Stalking seventh-grade homeroom,
hallways, gym class. *Your thick
glasses look ridiculous. Don't you wash
your face? Your pimples are disgusting.*

A probing mosquito-head seeking
soft openings. *Your hair is so greasy;
shouldn't you lose some weight?*
Every bully has reasons: father

who jumped ship, mother crumbling
at home, big sister giving the business—
gashing long nails, honing in on every slip,
every time I *looked like a fool.*

But now on top, with my own empire
of weirdos to gnaw on and peck. Antenna
for weakness, word skills to kill.
In my 30s, I met a classmate who told me

she'd never forgotten I said
she *would always be a loser.*
Heart sunk to my knees, I swore
apologies and told her I was nothing

like that anymore. But the sadness
was hers.

DREAM

I had my own Frankenstein monster he'd been
dormant I unwrapped him expecting him to lie
still but went away for a minute and he slid under my bed
I coaxed him out I'd been reading this book
about preemies being massaged by nurses' aides
so I started stroking his chest this soothed him
a big smile so happy he squeezed my tit
I told him to stop and relieved he did right away
his charred black face slowly turned marbled
blue I was scared but so glad to have a friend
who cared about me and maybe I should have a kid
whose limbs would shake and cry but I'd hug
and kiss him he'd reach his arms out and maybe grab
my cheek in greeting

MIAMI BEACH

*I'm sure if we had poets, they'd be writing about the swallowing
of Miami Beach by the sea.*

*—Bruce Mowry, Miami Beach city engineer, "The Siege of Miami,"
New Yorker, December 21 and 28, 2015*

Miami Beach is being swallowed by the sea. Pinks
and fuchsias drowned in turquoise sea-foam.
Water burbling up from limestone, salt
leaching into caipirinhas and mojitos.
Full moon slurry with tiki umbrella on top.

           My parents honeymooned
in Miami Beach—Versailles Hotel, 1955.
They had eaten the cake. Their 8mm
honeymoon reel first in our home movie box—
the sole brown canister in an ocean of grays and greens.
The one I rarely watched. Just them traipsing
on the beach, no kids, little to interest me.
Decomposing, I'm sure, in a closet
in my mother's house. Another film in need
of preservation.
           But not waterlogged,
not swallowed by the sea. That would be
Miami Beach. If a city and mortgage can be underwater,
so can a marriage. By the time I came along

it was already listing—money, sickness,
dad sleeping around. A 13-year groaning tilt,
till finally taken by the deep.

                      Then years
of bobbing up like a bloated corpse
for new rounds of hurt, recrimination,
crazy new girlfriends. Unsinkable—
the fester that wouldn't heal.

                    Miami Beach
is being swallowed by the sea.

GHOST LATITUDES

In the ghost latitudes, it's always confession time—
incessant ring of processional bells.

The future a rumor—
smudge splayed on a windshield.

Every road you take, shades
ride shotgun—

orbit your head like swings
fanning out

from an amusement ride's tower.
Ships tossed sideways by spectral winds,

from every corner of every map
hollowed cheeks blowing.

Today I saw Henry Kissinger on the subway

plotting to bomb Cambodia. Typing coordinates
on his iPad—Khmer scurrying

in the Arc Light. Carving a path for Pinochet.
Cabling Mao, giving Brezhnev

the slip. Scribbling a defense of Nixon,
TV makeup on gray statesman face.

Or maybe it wasn't Kissinger.
Just another owlish old man dreaming

of when the world was his briefcase.
Green the color of everything.

Power Out

I bought a double-wicked candle on a last-second
drugstore run. It wasn't on my list.

The two flames a furnace of light, I moved
through my apartment like a Medieval monk,

torch guiding my way from sleeping quarters
to study. Days weren't bad, but never such dread

of night. I tried to read, write, but cut off
in a barely lit apartment, solitude never felt so alone.

Went to a candle-lit bar but walking home
a dark dystopia, menace in every doorway.

So inside I stayed. Even after a couple of days
I'd walk into my bedroom, flick the useless switch.

I wish I could say a lover and I kept each other warm,
gamboled wild night after darkened night. But no.

Just candles and flashlights. I hardly bathed, but
when I could wait no more, the freeze rained down

my body. Breath sucked out, I managed to clean myself,
rinse my hair. And when I was done, water rattling

down the drain, I stood dripping, covered my face
and felt like—really wished—I could cry.

NATURE

Two birds doing it this morning
outside my window on top
of a rusted smoke flue.

She vibrates her tailfeather
up and down as if showing him
where to go. He gets on top of her

for a couple seconds, flutters
his wings and hops off.
Side of the ledge, he cleans his feathers,

looks in the distance, distracted. Acts
on his urge again—the force
of their union sends them tumbling

out of view. Don't know how successful
this coupling was, but judging
from the chirping it was a gas.

To me it didn't look like much fun—
brief, obligatory, violent.
Not that I've achieved

that trifecta. (I've achieved
that trifecta.) Not assault *violent*,
but desire doesn't try to be

on the side of the angels. *Brief*—
I've had issues. Pinatubo
in a New York minute; Vesuvio

as soon as you're in it. *Obligatory*—
when you're not sure
you want to stay, but not ready

to sever, so you continue
full-tilt electric, conceal
your sputtering feelings.

My mom said there was no warning
anything was wrong
right up to the day

my dad left, and she meant
in bed. She also said,
The apple doesn't fall far from the tree.

Meaning me.

Duck

One morning I was making coffee, pouring
hot water over grinds. I dumped the excess
into the sink and they settled into the perfect shape

of a duck. Darker concentration formed the beak,
speck for an eye—thin neck, round body, even
tail feathers. And I asked what had I done

to be so chosen? A perfectly ordinary morning,
but now this duck was in my sink and it must
mean something.

A Jesus-in-burnt-toast moment?
Annunciation? Had God been downsized
from ancient swan?

All I knew was that a duck was in my sink.
I wondered whether I should start
my own religion and get rich. L. Ron Hubbard

would know how to monetize this.
Mystical origin story, abstruse texts,
tie-ins, merch. Pilgrims flocking

to my fourth-floor walkup to see the duck
the scriptures predicted.
But I've never had a head for money,

and morning was galloping as mornings
do. Another cup to be made. I stayed
with the duck a while—used the bathroom sink

to wash my hands, rinse my mug.
But in the end, I let the faucet run
and the duck dissolved,

transubstantiating down the drain—
leaving me without blessing
or any new direction.

Borderline

For Christmas, you got me
the 45 of "Borderline."
And amid the tinsel and blinking lights,
we had a nice holiday. Behaved
perfectly civilized at your mother's house.
She made real cranberry sauce. I didn't know
it existed outside a can. We all had
a good laugh. Back to our place
and we might even have made love
that night.

        At no time did you
pace frantically around the apartment
because you lost your gray scrunchie,
forbidding me to touch or comfort you.
You did not visit me at work and kick me
in the parking lot because you thought
the busgirl was flirting with me.
Not once did you throw a humidifier
at me in the middle of the night,
follow me to my car in your nightgown
and drape yourself over the hood
to keep me from driving away.
When it seemed I'd really leave,

you didn't run to the kitchen, turn on
the gas and stick your head
in the oven. I did not pull you out
and hold you against the wall. The cops
didn't come soon after
because the super thought
I was beating you.

Keep pushing me
Keep pushing me
Keep pushing my love

Years later, on a therapist's couch,
she said *it sounds like she had*
Borderline Personality Disorder.
Which knocked me back—
a name, a condition for what
we lived through. Your pain.
My pain. Something I could Google,
investigate. Sunlight on the force
that, long after it passed, stalled
a wall cloud over my personal life.

Something in the way you love me
won't set me free.

"Borderline"—coiled in the living room
while we were in the midst of it.
Semaphore warning, but I didn't know
the signals. World War II grenade
discovered in a thrift shop—still armed,
still ready to go off.

WHAT YOU WISH FOR

My first memory is on a doctor's table—
post-convulsions. He examines me, gives
my parents a stack of tongue depressors

to take home. Wrapped in white tape,
as wide as my mouth—in case
I try to *swallow my tongue*. For years

the fear my tongue will offer itself
as lunch. But mostly content when sick,
my mom spooning me soup, rubbing Vicks

on my chest. Blessed attention, mother
and child union—no wish to stray or leap
ahead. As an adult so many times

at doctors' offices convinced of some grave
condition, but shakes of the head,
all *completely normal*. Part of me hoping the end

comes swift, sad. Waves of sympathy—
poor guy never saw it coming.

Picts

A tribe of Picts is fixing to cleave me.
Battle armor clanging, they close in,
tracking me over rivers and moors,
whipsawing around corners
of these halls. Through couriers
and shouts word has come down
of my treachery—slack ways,
squandered promise, my boat clinging
to shore.

       And this, the sentence
for my sins. Pikes raised, they fire their gaze
before they lunge. Azure-faced grins,
sword and pickaxe, they hack through
tendon and bone. No more need
for excuses. Shriven, free, I crumble
in a heap. Crimson permission to slow drain
my time.
       All mine, all mine.

Happy

I know things are going well for me when I'm choked
by fear of catastrophic illness. Liver failure from anti-

depressants, brain tumor from cell phones, lung cancer
from five years smoking. Sometimes I'm indifferent

to whether God's random jackhammer slams me down;
Jack Gilbert's *locomotive of the Lord* plows

through skin and bone. When you're trudging
through liquid amber, it's a relief to scuttle

the whole business. But when happy, I put hazard signs
around worksites, crossing gates and bells

along tracks. If the Lord came knocking in hardhat,
engineer overalls, I'd run.

Grocery/Covid

I plan trips with military precision,
know my targets like pins on a map—
more quartermaster than casual shopper.
Think how ridiculous it is that outside I zip
to the middle of the street to keep six feet
apart, while here, in cramped city aisles,
smoosh by people a mere foot away.
Past shoppers, past clerks stocking shelves,
doing God's work keeping a city eating—
virus ravaging their ranks. An old man
wobbles toward me—eyes flash anxious—
so I back out and wait till he's clear.
My glasses fog up from my mask
even though I did the shaving cream trick
my mother told me. My wheeled basket piles up
with a week's worth of shopping—salad, pasta,
soup, peanut butter, bananas. I navigate checkout
(no cash, no touch, no signature needed) and leave
the store with four heavy bags.

On the way in, I'd passed the Church of the Village,
people lined up around the block—for food, I think.
And now I'm carrying four bags of privilege
through emptied morning streets. My walk home

extended—I keep stopping because the weight's
too heavy for my arms. I imagine what I'd do
if a hungry stranger approached me with my haul.
*Here's an orange, a box of Triscuits, some wasabi
seaweed.* Sucking in heavy on my mask—I wish
I'd removed it, but remember I'm still passing people
on the sidewalk. I leave 14th Street and am back
in my leafy neighborhood. I lug the bags up to my walkup,
set them on the floor. Put goods away, wipe the counter,
then wash my hands with a thousand flames.
Safe, I go to my computer, google *Church of the Village
food bank.*

Palimpsest

The Pope asks the crowd to pray for him,
and says if any don't believe
or can't pray, send good wishes.

Well, who knows anymore? Somewhere
in me a Catholic boy remains.
Doctors say parts of a sibling or twin

left in the mother's womb might find their way
into the next born. Not born again. Trying
to find meaning in a without-God-meaningless world;

didn't Nietzsche say that? And even if I believe,
can I pray? God sets up the pins,
then lets the people bowl.

But will my desires sway him to guide
my ball into the sweet spot?
When I was a boy, I thought I was doing

God's work on earth—a good deed,
kind word, a smile. I like to think
I'm still the same, but for what purpose,

in whose name?

Vectoring

Circling over Chicago, burning fuel
so our plane's emergency landing
is only *somewhat overweight*.
Weather radar broken, not safe
to fly from New York to L.A.
Blowing through gas like mariners
once dumped cargo—wood, coal, livestock—
so sails could take wind again.
Only this time so we don't sail
through the runway.

Man next to me reading Recoil magazine—
for the gun lifestyle. My reaction
to the semi-automatics and belt clips
brings the title to life.
I'm reading a Louise Glück book, wondering
if my neighbor thinks—*snowflake*
poetry dude. But he seems like a nice guy—
gathering our row's used cups and trash
to give to the flight attendant.
Life is complicated.

Pilot says the landing gear will go down early
to burn more fuel; we'll be on the longest

runway at O'Hare. Ambulances and emergency
vehicles will be waiting for us.

If this is the end, should I strike up
a conversation with my neighbor?
Throw a rope bridge over the waters
that divide us? Last act to fill in the gap?
I don't. I mind my own, content to go down
cocooned in my head.

We land and two dozen fire trucks
and other vehicles greet us—each
flashing its angry halo.
We begin the slow winding down
of the flight. My neighbor packs
his magazine, reaches for his bag,
and wishes me a good day. I do the same.
I leave the plane and out
to the widening airport alone,
wondering where I'm going
to make my connection.

Aftermath

the only thing to do is simply continue
is that simple
yes, it is simple because it is the only thing to do
can you do it
yes, you can because it is the only thing to do

—*Frank O'Hara*

Catalogue all you resist
and call the wrecking crew
to the walls

When your ox is gored
on all sides
the kingdom isn't come

The confectioner has taken
his whisks and mixing bowls
clean out of town

I'd rain elegies
in sympathy but I've
become so

shallow lately
I screw my muse
to the sticking point

roll over and fall asleep
Unbuckle your holster
We'll broadcast our griefs

to the sky   Just because
I've sniffed out your tricks
doesn't excuse mine

Somewhere a mighty engine rumbles
a curtain is rent
But here the air's still

The ground a trembling silence
as scathed we set out again

Notes

"Walter S." is a found poem consisting of actual deposition
   testimony.

"Come Blow Your Horn" contains a line from the song "Come
   Blow Your Horn," written by Sammy Cahn and James van
   Heusen, performed by Frank Sinatra.

"Empire State Building, New York, 1967" contains the title of the
   Ramones' song "I Wanna Be Sedated."

"The Great Outdoors" references the artist Bruce Nauman's
   sculpture, "One Hundred Fish Fountain."

"Post-Parting" references the Beatles' song "Hey Bulldog," Neil
   Diamond's "Solitary Man," and Whitesnake's "Here I
   Go Again."

"Handheld" contains a line from the Elizabeth Bishop poem "Filling
   Station."

"Borderline" contains lines from the song "Borderline," written by
   Reggie Lucas, performed by Madonna.

"Happy" references the Jack Gilbert poem, "A Brief for the Defense."

"Aftermath" contains an epigraph from the Frank O'Hara poem
   "Adieu to Norman, Bon Jour to Joan and Jean-Paul."

Acknowledgments

There are just too many people to thank who have helped me along the journey that led to the publication of this book, but I'm going to give it a shot. Apologies in advance to anyone whom I might have overlooked.

I'll start by thanking the readers and editors of the following publications who originally published some of these poems, sometimes in slightly different form:

Black Rabbit Review, The Boiler Journal, Connotation Press—An Online Artifact, Ethel Zine, Flapperhouse, Indolent Books, Lyre Lyre, Mountain Gazette, On the Seawall, Prelude, Scapegoat Review, Scribble Magazine, Stone Highway Review, Triggerfish Critical Review, Voices in Italian Americana, and *Yes, Poetry.*

Martha Rhodes, who believed in me and took a chance on this book.

Ryan Murphy, Sally Ball, Hannah Matheson, Clarissa Long, and the whole wonderful team at Four Way Books.

Craig Morgan Teicher and David Wojahn, who provided invaluable assistance in sculpting these poems and piecing together this manuscript.

My family, especially my sisters—Rosemary, Donna, Joanne, and

Tricia—who helped create the memories and also helped to keep everything together. Love to you.

Ashley Hager—thank you, love, for changing everything for the better.

In memory of my father, Vincent Cappo.

In memory of my friend and early literary compatriot, Joseph Ramirez, a sweet soul who died too soon.

Sophia Starmack, Gregory Crosby, Abigail Welhouse, Joanna Valente, Joseph Quintela, Caitlin McDonnell, Carla Carlson, Kristina Andersson Bicher, Kate Knapp Johnson, Chris Hansen-Nelson, Andrea Bott, Matthew Thorburn, Jennifer Franklin, Micaela Bombard, Jessica Meade, Laura-Eve Engel, Leah Umansky, Cait Weiss, Miranda Field, Sharon Dolin, Melinda Wilson, Jen Fitzgerald, Lauren Sartor, Nicole Callihan, Liz Axelrod, Stefanie Lipsey, Bill Lessard, Ram Devineni.

Scott Kollman, Sylvester Wojtkowski, Mike Minervini, Nina Segal, Mark Evans, Harris Milman, Anne Carr Milman, Patrick Canavan, Lauren Block, Shona Gibson, Arsen Zartarian, Bill Flahive, Tim Burke, Joe Garemore, Jen Askling, Jeff Cohen, Ken Rivlin, James Carson, Mukesh Shah, Mike Sans, Jim Mussen, Emily Bauman, Joe Taras, Katerina Hager, Megan Sheffield.

The whole Hager-Ashley extended family—thank you for welcoming me with such open arms.

All of my Sarah Lawrence teachers, especially Dennis Nurkse, Victoria Redel, Marie Howe, Jeffrey McDaniel, Stephen Dobyns, Lorna Blake, and Kevin Pilkington. And all of my Sarah Lawrence classmates and workshopmates.

Some of these poems were created at, or inspired by, workshops at the following places (special thank you to Henri Cole at the New York State Summer Writers Institute, whose amazing prompts helped me write several of these poems):

Frost Place Poetry Conference
New York State Summer Writers Institute
Palm Beach Poetry Festival
Tin House Summer Workshop
Sarah Lawrence Summer Writing Seminars
Provincetown Fine Arts Work Center
Vermont College of Fine Arts Post-MFA Workshop
Juniper Summer Writing Institute, UMass Amherst
U.S. Poets in Mexico

And a big thank you to everyone for reading these pages.

Anthony Cappo is the author of the poetry chapbook, *My Bedside Radio*. His poems and other writings have appeared in *Prelude*, *The Rumpus*, *Thrush Poetry Journal*, *Yes Poetry*, and other publications. Anthony received his M.F.A. in creative writing from Sarah Lawrence College. He grew up in Cherry Hill, New Jersey, and now lives in New York City. His work can be found at anthonycappo.com.

Publication of this book was made possible by grants and donations. We are also grateful to those individuals who participated in our 2021 Build a Book Program. They are:

Anonymous (16), Maggie Anderson, Susan Kay Anderson, Kristina Andersson, Kate Angus, Kathy Aponick, Sarah Audsley, Jean Ball, Sally Ball, Clayre Benzadón, Greg Blaine, Laurel Blossom, adam bohannon, Betsy Bonner, Lee Briccetti, Joan Bright, Jane Martha Brox, Susan Buttenwieser, Anthony Cappo, Carla and Steven Carlson, Paul and Brandy Carlson, Renee Carlson, Alice Christian, Karen Rhodes Clarke, Mari Coates, Jane Cooper, Ellen Cosgrove, Peter Coyote, Robin Davidson, Kwame Dawes, Michael Anna de Armas, Brian Komei Dempster, Renko and Stuart Dempster, Matthew DeNichilo, Rosalynde Vas Dias, Kent Dixon, Patrick Donnelly, Lynn Emanuel, Blas Falconer, Elliot Figman, Jennifer Franklin, Helen Fremont and Donna Thagard, Gabriel Fried, John Gallaher, Reginald Gibbons, Jason Gifford, Jean and Jay Glassman, Dorothy Tapper Goldman, Sarah Gorham and Jeffrey Skinner, Lauri Grossman, Julia Guez, Sarah Gund, Naomi Guttman and Jonathan Mead, Kimiko Hahn, Mary Stewart Hammond, Beth Harrison, Jeffrey Harrison, Melanie S. Hatter, Tom Healy and Fred Hochberg, K.T. Herr, Karen Hildebrand, Joel Hinman, Deming Holleran, Lillian Howan, Thomas and Autumn Howard, Catherine Hoyser, Elizabeth Jackson, Jessica Jacobs and Nickole Brown, Christopher Johanson, Jen Just, Maeve Kinkead, Alexandra Knox, Lindsay and John Landes, Suzanne Langlois, Laura Lauth, Sydney Lea, David Lee and Jamila Trindle, Rodney Terich Leonard, Jen Levitt, Howard Levy, Owen Lewis, Matthew Lippman, Jennifer Litt, Karen Llagas, Sara London and Dean Albarelli, Clarissa Long, James Longenbach, Cynthia Lowen, Ralph and Mary Ann Lowen, Ricardo Maldonado, Myra Malkin, Jacquelyn Malone, Carrie Mar, Kathleen McCoy, Ellen McCulloch-Lovell, Lupe Mendez, David Miller, Josephine Miller, Nicki Moore, Guna Mundheim, Matthew Murphy and Maura Rockcastle, Michael and Nancy Murphy, Myra Natter, Jay Baron Nicorvo, Ashley Nissler, Kimberly Nunes, Rebecca and Daniel Okrent, Robert Oldshue and Nina Calabresi, Kathleen Ossip, Judith Pacht, Cathy McArthur Palermo, Marcia and Chris Pelletiere,

Sam Perkins, Susan Peters and Morgan Driscoll, Patrick Phillips,
Robert Pinsky, Megan Pinto, Connie Post, Kyle Potvin, Grace Prasad,
Kevin Prufer, Alicia Jo Rabins, Anna Duke Reach, Victoria Redel,
Martha Rhodes, Paula Rhodes, Louise Riemer, Sarah Santner,
Amy Schiffman, Peter and Jill Schireson, Roni and Richard Schotter,
James and Nancy Shalek, Soraya Shalforoosh, Peggy Shinner,
Anita Soos, Donna Spruijt-Metz, Ann F. Stanford, Arlene Stang,
Page Hill Starzinger, Marina Stuart, Yerra Sugarman, Marjorie and
Lew Tesser, Eleanor Thomas, Tom Thompson and Miranda Field,
James Tjoa, Ellen Bryant Voigt, Connie Voisine, Moira Walsh,
Ellen Dore Watson, Calvin Wei, John Wender, Eleanor Wilner,
Mary Wolf, and Pamela and Kelly Yenser.